CHRONICLES
OF
A SURVIVOR

Written by Ackeisha Kimberly Kent

ISBN: 9781973439769

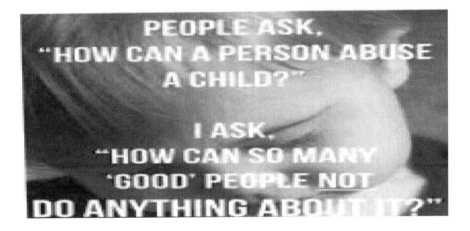

PEOPLE ASK, "HOW CAN A PERSON ABUSE A CHILD?"

I ASK, "HOW CAN SO MANY 'GOOD' PEOPLE NOT DO ANYTHING ABOUT IT?"

This book is dedicated to my life story, enduring and surviving abuse!

It was written for the millions of little girls and boys out there, going through, or who have experienced, child sexual abuse, or any kind of abuse. It would have thrown their lives into chaos and caused them so much pain and suffering. This book was written with love, compassion, tears and hope! It was written to let you, my dear readers, know that there is always a light at the end of the tunnel, that you are not alone! There are people who are willing to be your voice!

Once you take the first step to break the silence, that is where you truly start to heal!

I am the Voice of the Voiceless!

"When Silence is Broken the True Strength of a Survivor is Born!"
#iStandwomensmovement #chroniclesofasurvivor
#strongwomen #survivors #boysandgirlseverywhere
#voiceofthevoiceless

Written by: Ackeisha Kent

Chapter 1

Why me??

I was barely ten years old when it all started a little girl who only wanted the love and attention of a father. I was full of life and all I wanted to do was play with dolls and have fun with my other brothers and sisters. There were six of us at that time, but seemed like my father had other plans! While I was slowly developing he was wickedly creating my world of doom! It started late one night as I slept on a small couch in my room. My little sister slept peacefully on the floor, on a mattress, while my father stood over me and fondled me. I was confused as to what was happening and why. Tears streaming down my cold cheeks he led over and whispered into my ears, "If you ever tell your mother I will beat you!" Anyone who knows Barry Kent knows a beating from him was not one you would wish on your worst enemy!
This went on for a while the touching, fondling and the threats! I was so afraid of him that when I heard his name, my heart would race, I'd jump or disappear into my room.

The Mosque!

Where was God I asked?

We became Muslims at one point. At that time, my father thought having the Mosque under our house would be nice. I guessed so too, but I was wrong again. My dad had other plans. His intentions were never good. Being a Muslim was fun and had its up times like 'games for prizes' and get-togethers. These were a few of the good times I had as a Muslim girl. I didn't tell the Imam, nor the other heads, what was going on, for fear that my father would find out what I was saying about him and his actions! So, I stayed quiet through these times. I would talk and laugh and still win all the tests given in our sessions. I got my prizes every time and everything seemed normal to the naked eye. I believe people only see what they want to see and once something doesn't affect them, they are hardly ever ready to lend assistance or stand up for what is right. My father was perceived as a good man, to some, and in little Tobago a man will kill to hide his sins! So, I endured the nights he would wake me up when everyone else was sleeping and take me downstairs in what was supposed to be the mosque and sexually molest me and take advantage of my innocence and body! I guess that's what the mosque was for, because we didn't remain Muslim for long.

Eventually As my darkness grew darker and the windows of hope started fading, I started to believe that it has to be something about me that was causing my dad to ill-treat and abuse me this way! I was slowly disappearing into a figment of myself. I would dread the nights for the mere thought of what it brings. Night's for me were most times spent waiting. Waiting for the animal I called dad! I could remember the first time my father ask me "stick it in". It was one of the most stink things he had ever done, but by far not the worst! My response to him was, "No!" He proceeded to play with his penis by my vagina, whilst fondling my tiny breasts, until he excreted! Still that wasn't enough, as the abuse matures in nature the licks and molestation was no match for what was to come!

I started seeing my menstruation and then the missing of cycles began! There was one time, actually the first time I missed my period, he asked me if my monthly came. I said, "No." He immediately told me to write the name of a tablet known for having abortions, Cycotec, on a paper and gave me money to go to the drug store to buy it. I did as I was told and returned. I was then told to drink the tablets and later that day I was asked again if my period came down. I replied, "No." I was then asked if I had eaten anything for the day. I said, "Yes," which followed with a box across my cheeks and his cursing, "You stupid! You ent know you not supposed to eat?" The tears streamed down my cheeks. I didn't know, after all, I didn't have a boyfriend and I wasn't having sex with anyone else, so how would I know that, at such a tender age.

The verbal abuse, physical abuse and beatings continued anytime I slipped and so did the sexual molestation. My mom was always busy, and if not busy, tired! So he knew when she retired for the night, she was out till next morning. So, the nights were his. The nights the real monster came out to play. I recall, as though it were yesterday, the dirty feeling I felt at that time.

There was one time that monster, I called dad, placed his mouth on my vagina and was sucking it. Ughh, it felt so icky and nasty, it made me feel even more dirty than I was already used to feeling. The next day he asked me how it felt. I said I did not know and he started to choke me in the corner of the doorway. I gasped for breath. Tears ran out my eyes as I thought, this is it, sure death. I didn't die that day, even though at that time I wished for it!

Fortnight Fridays: I Am Not for Sale!

Every fortnight I was treated to some of daddy's money. I was paid as though I was his little whore. I was always the first to go to his bank account since he'd give me his card and tell me to go check to see if his pay had arrived. I would do as I was told and return home. I would be given three hundred dollars, sometimes more, but I knew what the dirty money was for. Since I was daddy's toy, with that money, also came the sick feeling of what was to come at nightfall.

He made me feel like I had no worth. Most nights, or days, when he came I wished death would rescue me... but death never came.

Chapter 2

The Beatings

I remember the licks... every stroke, every sound from the tambran whip.

Daddy spared no one! Every brother and sister knew the taste of his whip and nursed the bruises from the water hose, cutlass or tambran whip.

I believed we all disliked daddy, but for me it was more than dislike, it was hate and disgust.

I was slowly going crazy in my mind, at least that's how I felt. Then one day I decided that I was going to end it all, end him.

That day was a normal day like any other, but it was the day I was planning to kill him.

Yes, I was so fixated on my dream of wanting him to go away, that I decided that I'll do it myself.

He called for his usual glass of water or juice and there I had the perfect opportunity to strike. Armed with my rat poison I started to mix it in, not noticing that my kid sister was in the corridor watching. Before I knew it, she rushed in knocking the glass of juice into the sink. I was furious, but I couldn't make a scene. I know she had seen me cry many times before. She also heard me say I was being hurt by daddy but I don't think she understood what it meant at the time.

She never told daddy though. If she had, I'm sure today, I would have been no more. See, daddy was also a violent man. His bite was worse than his bark and so was his hand. You would have never wanted to get him angry, because with his anger came pain, fury, sorrows and worries.

Chapter 3

My first car accident !!

Why was daddy taking me to Crown Point side instead of Calder Hall that Sunday morning? See, in the midst of all my pains and sorrows I still chose to believe that one day I'd be Free. That fateful Sunday morning I was about to leave for church when daddy said he'd drop me. My heart sank as thoughts started to rush through my head. My heart began to race as my body began to shake, trembling inside as I waited, as I anticipated, his next sick move. I had an idea of what was next. I started to think about the dirty sticky feeling I have whenever I was around daddy. Immediately I started to feel funny. This weird feeling swept over me as though something within me knew that things were about to get worse. We left shortly after mummy gave daddy his morning cup of tea. The keys in the ignition... voom voom... and my father drove off, but where was he taking me? The direction of my church was Calder Hall, Wesleyan Holiness Church, I noticed he wasn't taking me in that direction. Instead he was heading towards Crown Point, but I guess the Lord had other plans for me that day. I guess the Lord knew that if he'd reached his destination something terrible, something worse than that which I was enduring, was going to happen. So, He stopped it. That's what I thought. As daddy proceeded past the Lowlands and speeded up to Hampden Road opposite Cads Junction another vehicle came flying out from the side street and made impact with my dad's car. Our car swerved and was heading, head on, into the bus shed. I guessed daddy wasn't ready to die, he pull away from the bus shed and screechhh... bang into the poui tree. I wasn't injured in anyway but daddy head was burst, split open at the centre of his forehead. I felt nothing for him. My only thought, at that time, was I wish he had died. Part of me wished I had died that day also. I was tired. I was fed-up. I felt as though I couldn't go on.

That day was a dramatic one. Police to take accident report. Ambulance and all the attention from passers-by. This commotion made me angry because in all the drama happening, no one, no one saw my pain, my cry! The silent cries of a young girl. No one could hear the screams and voices in my head. No one! At the end of it all daddy got his stitches and his car fixed in the following weeks. For the next two weeks, the atmosphere at home was a weird one. Everyone was in their own world as daily routines went on as normal.

My childhood didn't have much fun memories, except for the few good friends I had in school. I attended the Scarborough R.C. School where I met my best friends Isha, Giselle and Shivva. These girls and I all met at different levels throughout my primary school days. Those days where the good ole days.

Shivva and Giselle were my girls from Std 1 to Std 5. Isha we met in Std 4, but the bond we had and the memories we shared will live on in my heart forever.

There were days when I would go to school with only a cup of hot water tea in my stomach and not even a penny in my pocket but I was never left without, once these girls had. We would walk to and from school together. Most afternoons we would stop in the botanical gardens and play. Sliding on palm leaves we called them boats "laughing" these little things were what made me happy growing up in an unhappy home where abuse crept in and destroyed my young life.

Of all my friends, when I met Isha I immediately bonded with her plus we had known each other from before since we both grew up in Scarborough, and attend the same church at that time, Victory Outreach.

We got much closer as we were now in the same Std 4 class. We started walking to school together sometimes and that gave us time to play, chat and have fun along the way!

Chapter 4

Speaking about the abuse for the first time!

I eventually trusted her enough to tell her what was happening to me. She was angry and shocked by what I was telling her. When I started telling her how my dad comes into my room at night and fondles me, she told me she was sick to her stomach. She was angry and she too wished he was dead. It's was around this time my life started to change. No, not for the better, but for the worse. She started to advise me, telling me I should go to the police or something, because what he was doing to me was wrong. I didn't take her advice though and so the incest continued. I was afraid. Afraid of what my dad would have done to me if he got to know that I was even thinking about going to the police. I eventually confided in my bigger sister who had returned from living in Trinidad, telling her what was happening at home. It was then that action started to take place. By then I was in Std 5 and waiting on results from my Common Entrance exam, to enter Secondary school. My big sister Keisha took me to the Social Services. This was where issues dealing with incest and abuse against children was dealt with. We were assigned a social worker, a female, and from there I started speaking out about my abuse. There were a series steps that we had to take before anything was done. They had to get all the details from me of all the incidents of abuse I could remember while they took their notes. I had to go to the police station's Child Protection Unit and make an official report which I did with my sister's help and support. The police took their report. Then I was taken to the hospital, to test to see if I was tampered with sexually. The reports confirmed I was being interfered with. By this point I was terrified as the tides were closing in on the police making an arrest. A part of me was happy, but the other part was very much afraid. I started to think what would happen to me if my dad was arrested and then released on bail or something. What will become of me when he got those filthy hands on my frail developing body.

But there was no going back now. The police were ready to move.

My mom just had my little sister. She was so tiny and barely a few weeks old when the dreaded day came. It was a Monday afternoon. Everyone was already home from school and about the village or at home. My brothers were not at home as they were always roaming the streets either looking for trouble or creating trouble! My mom and dad were both inside the house. I was downstairs as I knew what was about to happen that evening. I didn't want to be close to my father's sight when it happened.

Chapter 5

The Arrest!

I heard the good afternoon call and I jumped to my feet and ran to the back of the house, as I heard my dad's voice answer, "Who is that?" His footsteps echoed as he walked towards the porch to the front door.

I knew my mom would have followed as usual. "Like a puppy always behind this fool," I muttered to myself. I listened quietly to what the police were saying. They told him they had a warrant for his and my mom's arrest for abuse against one of his daughters Ackeisha. I heard my mom cry out and my father cursed as they took them both away in hand cuffs. That's good, right? Well I guess so. Only, under the circumstances, there was also a helpless baby laying in the house, my little baby sister! My helpless baby sister, so innocent and so cute.

My problems were now beginning... the boys I knew as brothers were not happy with me and I was not happy with myself. I thought that my mom would not have been arrested since I didn't tell her what was happening to me and most times she was either sleeping, not around because she travelled, or just about the house and hard doing her duties. I was torn! I was happy, for one part but sad for the other. My mom was innocent in this, I believed, and my brothers started to threaten me to get their father out of jail or they would deal with me. The happiness and peace I thought would come from my dad paying for his sins was turning out to be more than I could handle. I started to think of how I could undo what I did if not for myself for my baby sister and my mother who I loved dearly. My mom came out on bail the next day and she was questioning me but wasn't ready to believe me. As usual mummy took the easy way out. So, I now began to believe, and wonder, if she really knew and turned a blind eye since daddy was the bread winner of the family.

Mummy did all she could do to get him out of the cell over the next days. While she was looking for ways to get the devil out his cell, I was busy plotting my escape from my cell where I was facing hell. All I knew is that I wanted to be gone by the time he got out.

After all, I told the police that I made up everything. That was the only way to get things to work out for him to get out of jail. I had to keep saying that, "My abuse never happened." You know doing this was the only way I could save my mum from going to prison and by doing that it helped to free my perpetrator as well. The worst feeling, I have ever felt, was that feeling of disgust at myself for having to lie and recant the actual truth. It was the only way I thought I could protect my mum, so she could be around to take care of my one-month-old baby sister and other siblings.

Once I did all that I needed to do, I was taken to Trinidad by my mum to stay with my aunt, mummy's elder sister Adora!

A New Start! My first time living in Trinidad!

I was happy at last! For a while everyone was happy, I guess. Daddy was out of jail and so was mummy. My brothers got what they wanted which was for me to get their father out of prison and I was living with my aunt. A new start, a new home and soon I'd start a new school.

My aunty Adora was a nice, but firm, Christian woman. Living with her was also my little cousin Akiel and my elder cousin Trudy. We all got along well. I eventually started school again about 2 weeks later, Bishops Centenary High School.

Chapter 6

New School!!!

Bishops Centenary High School was an all-girls school and so the distraction of boys wasn't there and I was happy. I made new friends, walked to and from school. We even had each other over at our houses and I was introduced to some of their wonderful parents. This sometimes made me wonder why I didn't have parents like my friends. This feeling of lack... of parental love started to fill my head. I started to feel somewhat inferior to my mates. I started to feel sad, alone, angry and filthy! To the extent to wanting to kill myself. Oh how I thought about my death so many times, those days were dark. I started to pull away and seclude myself from some of my friends and stopped talking to anyone at home. This was it. I had found myself in a dark place once again.

I was sad. I was broken. I was depressed. Why was my life this way? Why was I always hurting and in pain?
Why am I here? What is my purpose?
Is this what God has planned for me? No! In my heart, I refused to accept that ...but it was my sad reality.
As the months went by I slowly degenerated into a figment of myself. I was so unhappy and alone in my world. Then one day about four months later my mom came to take me back home.

Yes, back home to the place where it all started. She said my dad had moved on from everything that happened and is not angry. I laughed because I knew that my dad never let go of anything! Especially when he thinks that he did nothing wrong or just out of pure ignorance. He will keep things and when you least expect it, in anger, you will hear all you thought he has forgotten. My father was a tyrant of a man.

I had no say or choice in the matter, since they had already decided. They also concocted a story that my aunt was trying to turn me against my father and family. It was so funny to see how a person can manipulate people into believing their lies and evil plans. I will go, because I had no choice. I went because I had no say. I was already in a dark place and frankly I didn't care.

Chapter 7

Back to where I started!

I returned to Tobago with my mom and back where my father wanted me. My father barely had much to say to me for a few weeks, but I could see the fury in his eyes when I watched him at times. I could feel his anger and I knew he was only putting on a show. He eventually told me that he was sorry if he ever wronged me. Sorry if he hurt me. Seemed to me that he still didn't accept the fact that he did hurt me. How could he, how dare he say "if" he hurt me. That was the only so-called apology I ever got!

One day mommy came and told me that she would be sending me for spiritual cleansing. "What! Spiritual cleansing for what exactly," I screamed in my head. "Was she crazy?!" Who came up with this and convinced her that I had spiritual problems or that I'm being attacked by spirits? I guess that's why no one in my immediate family believed me. Yet all that had been happening to me was true! To make matters worse, I had convinced the police that I lied so the matter was closed now. I was labelled as a child possessed by evil spirits that was telling lies and making up stories.

The day finally came and mummy sent me to meet this man. He was a family friend on my mother's side of the family. Manni was an evil man. He had his work on the port and he was playing obeah man on the side. Manni would light candles and say prayers while he made me lay naked on a dirty piece of mattress in a tiny room across from the market. He would say to me, "The same way the spirits entered you, the same way they must exit." He would then proceed to have intercourse with me, a thirteen-year-old little girl. I guess mummy is to blame for being so stupid. She listened to such crap and exposed her daughter, to such an evil man who only added to her sexual abuse. This happened a few times before. When it stopped, the regular abuse started again.

I remember the times mummy use to send me to drop food for daddy down by the popular 'Store Bay Beach' in Crown Point. It was a beautiful beach. People from everywhere who visited Tobago had to visit Store Bay Beach. There were craft booths all around and eateries across the facility. My father also rented a craft booth there.

I remember how angry I used to feel each time I had to go to drop food, not because I didn't want him to eat but because I knew when I got there he would want to touch or feel me. It was sick. It was nasty and wicked of him, the things he use to do to me.

There was one time a Saturday I went to drop food as usual that day as I arrived at the beach I saw a few of my neighbourhood friends and so I was happy. So I decided to ask my dad of I could go down and bathe on the beach. Of course, he said yes... one plot to keep me around till his closing in the evening. I went down to the beach and got into the blue salt water where my friends were already swimming and having fun. As I got into the excitement I was free for just a moment! That moment quickly disappeared as I got under water. For an underwater swim, one of the boys there, decided to pull out his penis and shake it in front my face under the water! I flew up with a fury as I started to lay out curses on him, "How dare you! You sick, nasty stinking pervert!" I let him have it, then I left angry as I stormed back to the shore and up to my father's booth.

As I got closer to my dad's booth I tried to put on a normal face. I was not in the mood to answer any stupid questions he might have and decided to ask. I then quickly went to the restroom bathe off the salt water and returned to the booth once again. I told my dad that I was ready to go home, only for him to tell me we will go together when he closes up. My heart started to pound because I knew that meant he wanted to fondle me before we got home. He just had to satisfy his sick craving to abuse his daughter. This went on for a few months, on and off, until I decided at thirteen years old to run away from home.

Chapter 8

Running Away from home!

Each day as I left for school I would carry away a piece of my clothes and I would drop it off at my first boyfriend's sister's house.

By this time they had already known that I was being abused since I had opened up to his big sister and younger sister Lee who was also my girlfriend. They didn't mind me coming to live with them after all I was already being abused and I would be more happy and comfortable staying at their house. Matt, my childhood boyfriend and first boyfriend was a great guy. He never took advantage of me. Our times spent together at that time was passed with us cuddling, talking, laughing and watching BET Music videos or movies. Those were some good times! I remember the first time we both cooked together, giggling. We made fried scrambled eggs and bread. The hot oil splashed and burn the top of his red nose. I laugh as I remember! It wasn't anything big. He just got a little red bladder spot, like the red nose reindeer! It was a great day! The best I had in years!

It was also the day I decided to have sex with him for the first time. Since I was already being interfered with by my dad, why not with the boy I liked? At that time I still thought naively that I was a virgin, since I cannot remember if my dad ever really stuck it in. He had asked few years before that, when I was ten years old. You see that day, that faithful day, my deepest fear came true. That day, I knew for sure, I was not a virgin. That day I had to accept the reality that my flower was already plucked... by my father. That day when I had sex for the first time at thirteen years old, I didn't feel a thing. I did not bleed in anyway. I didn't even feel slight pain or discomfort. But how? Of all the books I read, of all the information my mom told me on the subject... you mean I really wouldn't have felt anything? No!

Matt said to me, that day, Keisha you are not a virgin! I can remember the rain pouring in the rooftop as I started to cry I cried because I knew who took my flower! I cried because I was ashamed! Matt tried to comfort me by saying, "It's ok! It doesn't change how I feel. You're still my girl!" Matt was such a nice boy. He was the first boy to ever give me a birthday gift, jewellery at that! So we had something special, though we were young.

For the rest of that week I would sit and my mind would travel to the most evil places. My mind, consumed with so many dark thoughts, of how to get rid of my wicked father! That week I remembered every evil act that was inflicted upon me. Every bad word spoken to me. Every cut ass I got for no reason. Every time he made me take that tablet, "Cycotec!" For every bad thing, that week, I premeditated upon him. Only vengeance and hate filled in my heart. How could he have done this? How could he have broken his daughter in this way. Of course my mom would eventually find me and take me back home and my short-lived happiness would disappear again. I would return home, take my licks and my curses, and as usual things will go silent for a while then start again.

One day my mom was downstairs cooking and she sent me to carry a glass of water for my dad which he had earlier called for. I was reluctant to go carry that water I knew him too well. I could sense it coming. But like any teenager, or child, I had no choice. When I got upstairs and gave him the water, he rested it down on the floor and came towards me. He said let me burst that bump on your cheek. Bump on cheek? Well the bump ended up being on my chest. It was indeed a bump, but that bump was my little breast. As he was fondling them, my mom burst through the curtain from the porch to enter the living room and asked, "What's this? What's going on here?" My dad being as slick and conniving as he was, had already pull his hand out from in my top. Playing he 'squeezing bump on my face' laughing now. He quickly said, "Nothing, I am just bursting a button on her face," and my mom swallowed that lie up! "What a fool," I thought in my head. "Didn't she see?" I asked myself. No! She couldn't Have.

I believed my mom did try, since I can remember her leaving at one point, but that was short lived. He found her and brought us all back home.

By this point I was really rebelling. I wanted out! All I knew is that people in the outside looking in didn't know how I felt. The pains I have to endure, the beatings, the touching, the fondling. They just didn't know, and even if they did, I often wondered, 'would they even care?' The mentality of most is, 'If it isn't me, I'm good!' No you're not good. One day I'll seep through the cracks, into your own home, then you'll know! You see the little island I grew up in called 'bago.' I believe that people believed that these things should be kept a secret, or dealt with within the family. However, I believed and still believe, that silence is what helped to force me, into the cold arms, of the open world.

By the end of that year I was just wandering through my days. I would walk the streets talking to myself as though I was going mad. I would talk to myself and not even be aware that I was doing it. People were beginning to notice. One day my mom told me that someone said they saw me walking and talking to myself. It looked like something was bothering me, but as usual I told her, "Nothing. I'm fine. I had long accepted the fact that there was nothing she could do, so I won't bother to stress her, or tell her anything. Nothing will change anyway. All I knew was, I was planning to leave again and this time I was not coming back no matter what! I started to strengthen my mind that, whatever I faced this time, I will not let them find me ...nor would I return home. I rather die out in the cold, bitter, brutal world! Meanwhile I saved any little cash I got my hands on and I waited. I waited for the next opportunity to make my big escape! My birthday wasn't far away... fifteen years old. I was getting closer. March month was finally here and I turned fifteen. With that birthday, also was a well-planned way in how I would leave and where I would go. I had a friend living in Signal Hill that I would stay by until I decided my next move. with that plan I was ready. It was a late Friday night in May everyone was asleep and it was my time to take my leave I had packed a bag earlier that night with as much cloths and shoes I could carry, along with the cash I had saved; and I sneaked out quietly into the dark night. I got out the yard and headed for the taxi stand walking with my head down so as not to be made out by anyone who may know me. It wasn't long before I got to my friend D's house, when I got there his family were asleep also and so it was easy for him to take me in without any questions he said he'd deal with that the next day. His mom was cool though she felt for me when she heard my story and she was scared for her son since he was older than I was but she allowed me to stay none the same after he had done some pleading on my behalf. I knew D liked me and I liked him too since Matt had migrated to England and he was nice and kind to me more than the guy I use to call my boyfriend at the time. D and I bonded he understood me and he was not in any hurry to have sex with me! That made me like him more I felt respected by him so I ended what friendship I had with Shane and got to knew D better. It was worth it we had something good going we connected on another level, I spent about three months by D before my dad bounced us up one day walking in town and told me I had till 8pm that day to come home! I had already made my stand on that I will not return I said in my head ' as he drove off , I knew I had to leave I started to not feel safe I told D that I feel he knows where I was staying and I didn't want what he has done in pass to happen so I would leave!, D was worried but I was terrified I just wanted to disappear so I decided that night that the next day I would take the boat to Trinidad that was the only place he couldn't reach me. And so I packed my bags again and did as I had said the next day I left for Trinidad. I was so afraid even while I was boarding the vessel I was looking around just to make sure my dad was nowhere to be seen. When I boarded the boat I was unhappy and I was hurting I sat in a corner by a table and I cried, and cried thinking what was next where was I going and what was my fate. Whatever it was I would embrace it, it couldn't be worse than what I was already going through or home through over my young years.

Chapter 9

Freedom! - Oh So I Thought

I remember vividly it was an experience I will Never forget; I left home from Tobago to Trinidad 15years old and Alone in a sea filled with sharks; and evil all around, it was a Sunday in the month of March 2003! I cannot remember the day, I boarded the ferry thinking oh yes, I am free, free from pain, free from my own cries, free from myself, free from hurt! Or so I thought ▯ young, naive, hurt, confused and angry I had willed myself to take the leap "a better life"- that was the idea, the plan. But what did I know huh? , what did I really know? The ferry sailed and on the journey, I met a man, hmmm oh how he made me feel safe when he started to speak to me about Jesus! yes be careful of some of those men and women that coming telling you about Jesus these people can also be the Devil! ...., the good news of hope in Jesus in my turmoil sounded great, he asked me questions and I answered, the conversations went on and on; now me not knowing where I was going to sleep or what I was going to eat when I get to Trinidad was on my mind, when this man asked, where will I be going after I got off the boat, I responded I was not sure but I was sure that his God will provide. Oh that must have been the answer he wanted to hear! he quickly offered me a place to stay in the popular Curepe area, so God do answer prays I thought! - p.s. God does Answer Prayers.

I got to Trinidad boat docked and we were off, he took me to the place and told me he doesn't live there only does his woodwork business there; and rents elsewhere, that was even better I thought! he helped me settle in then left!

Oh what a great man I thought. days went by until I saw him again, he said he wanted me to settle in and he will check me daily to chill and make sure I was ok.

That's good Right! "NO!

That was just the beginning of what was going to be a nightmare ending!

Chapter 10.

The Nightmare! story continues... 15yrs old and Raped!

this man appeared to be a blessing in disguise, I thought that was a good person and wanted to honestly help me after hearing some of my life story, while journeying from Tobago to Trinidad a week back, short space of time for someone to start changing on you Right!? , well he did! as the first week went by I noticed, he was starting to really show up every day like he had said, only now he started to lay down rules, he didn't want me bringing anyone there and he also said that soon I will have to start to pay!, now at this point I started to watch him different and decided to go looking for a little job to pay like he had mentioned. After looking and asking at several cloths and shoes store that day, I retired for the day leaving the last location I applied to for a sales clerk position in POS, I was tired, hungry and had a banging headache, with limited cash remaining from what I had I only remained with enough to get me back to Curepe and to where at the time was called home!.

When I got there that devil was waiting!, I slowly walked in said good evening, he responded and then asked me where I had been, I said job hunting but I was too tired and had a headache to talk. He told me as I walked off to the room that he had pain killers in his workshop outside for when he got any pains and he will go get 2 for me, I said thank you and continued to the room; I changed and returned to the living room for the tablets, at this point I am feeling weak because I didn't eat anything and didn't want to ask him for any money, when he returned shortly after I took the clear bag which had 4 small white tablets in it, I quickly got some water and I drank two, only two of those seemingly harmless pills!, and in less than a few minutes I started to feel light-headed and somewhat drowsy, so I walked towards the room mumbled thanks and I laid down. I don't know what happened next, or how soon after it happened, but I know that when I opened my eyes ⬚ the next day it was almost 12noon in the day and my belly was paining, my vagina was feeling pain, slimy stick grime from that beast running down my legs, the only thing I didn't do that day was killed myself, I screamed, I cried, I was in a distorted mess! I REALLY DID PAY!

Chapter 11

Leaving the House of Rape!

I left the #HouseOfRape, the following day, after waiting around for that bastard to show his demonic face! but he never showed.... like the guilty he wasn`t one to return to the scene of his crime. I never saw him again, so I left with my scars and pains, I Left! to a place unknown -the Streets! I no longer felt safe, I felt like if I was drifting; like I was in a place with darkness all around me, yes it was at this point I started to lose myself, it was at that point I said to myself that Nobody cares, it was at this point I realized even more so how evil the world really is, and I didn't care anymore!...

wandering around the curepe area for 3 good days I bounced into an ole friend of a friend from Tobago, and I told her part of what had happened she decided to allow me to stay with her till I got somewhere to go/stay. - my 1st escape from the horrors of the street, and I thank God that he was with me even though it may not have seemed like it at that time back then, but trust me something Mightier than myself was at work.... but like all my other lucky circumstances this housing was short lived!, I started looking for work again and I would leave home just like my friend and return after job hunting, only to return one day about two weeks into my stay to find the lock on her door broken and everything trashed upside down in her little room!, of course she blamed me and asked me to leave her room she didn't care where I went she just wanted me to leave !, so I would leave and return to the street I made up my mind that I would make it one or another but return home and returning to Tobago was not an option. I cried my tears while walking until I got to the corner by royal castle in curepe I went in Sat at one of the tables and I sobbed I didn't realize that a man was observing me until someone sat in the chair across from me and said, 'why are you crying' I answered that my friend had thrown me out and I had nowhere to go.

Chapter 12

The Escort Service

He then offered me a place to stay and asked if I wanted a job? I quickly agreed and said yes all I was really studying was that I would have a place to stay a roof over my head and a job though I didn't know what the job entailed he said that it was to just go out with rich men or business men to functions or house parties etc. that sounded fairly ok nothing much right?!

Wrong there was more to the job than what met the eyes more than what he had told me! And I would come to rude awakening a few days later when the boss John said he had to test or sample the goods to make sure that it was good or might I say quality lol hmmm the sick men it has in this world you'd never know until you encounter them. What could I do I had nowhere to run nowhere to go and two strapped men also in the house with other girls as well! , I knew there was no way out I had already stayed in there housing, eaten their food and started to become friends with the other girls. So I did what I had to do I allowed him to sample to touch and have sex with me that was the start of my escort days that was where I was stripped of all my dignity and pride as a young lady and you know what at that point I no longer cared again. Everything was taken from me so why should I care about me when all I seemed to know, experience and feel was pain!

I finally was called upon to go out on my first job which was to dance with a group of girls at a house party, Princess and Mary my two closest friends at that time were also at this house party, when we all got there we were welcomed by a house full of men, a house full of sharks, waiting to devour fresh meat. They all look like a bunch of sick perverts to me but who cared! We were shown the room to undress, washroom and table to the alcoholic drinks! After all they wanted us to" free up!" one man said, another laughed while others were skimming the room looking for their favourite pick! The music was blasting an the party was in full swing one of the girls Sparkle she could real dance, so she went upon she head and had the men going crazy who was touching her was calling her and who wasn't calling her name was busy fondling another in the dark corners, I was in the midst flexing on a guy who had be lock down as though I was his woman, while dancing he would feel up my body and with the alcohol in my system anything was prone to happen, the last thing I remember from that party was leaving next morning!, I woke up on a bed with two other girls and banging headache. I didn't ask any questions I knew that sex had taken place and that was part of the job so I woke up the other girls we got ready to leave there was only two men at the house that morning, so before we left he asked if we wanted anything to eat I replied no, immediately and started walking towards the door and so the others followed. We walked out the road and got into a maxi taxi back to San Juan. When we got home our boss was already there waiting, as we break the door he asks how was it??, I laughed and walked off to the room, what stupid question was that? how the help was it supposed to be? In my head I wanted to slap the stupid out of him! But I was no match for John, my small frame cannot do anything to him. When the other girls came into the room they had their cut in the night's earnings and said that John said I can come for mines, I got up and went out to the living room where John was still sitting and stretched out my hand to collect my earning he asked why I was reacting that way I asked him if he had a daughter of he would send her to do the things he was using other people's daughters to do for money? That angered John as he answered no! You are John knew what he was doing was wrong, he knew he was taking advantage of young helpless girls and he just didn't care. It's a jungle out there, and in that world in that kind of life there are many dangers! There was another time I was sent out on a job this time I was alone, and the guy decided that on his way to God knows where! he would pick up his partner.

Now we all know that when a guy picks up other male friends when going on a beat that there is more planned than what may meet the eye, and oh he had something plan alright, I knew something was wrong I knew my life was in danger but there was no escape in sight. As the car continues driving the drive seemed like eternity I was thinking what will I do when the car finally comes to a stop! I thought I would have no other choice than to make a run for it!, I had to escape because I feared for my life I couldn't endure another Rape! . When the car finally stopped I noticed it was in the vicinity of a river so my next thoughts and hope was that there would be somebody or people by the river that day at least that would deter them from their sinister plans and save me. As we walked up the river bank the place was quiet and there was no sign of human life or activity there, my heart sank as I quickly scanned my brain for another plan! But while doing that one of the guys said let's stop here, and told me to take off my clothes I was terrified and I did as I was told I took off my pants and my underwear and then I was told that I should give the guy who hired me friend a blow job while he the one who paid for me had sex with me I objected I said my boss told me is one person I am to engage with, and I started to scream!! I am saying kill me! kill me! In that second I was ready to embrace the cold arms of death; because I was not about to give in to his orders. I could suddenly hear voices in the distance someone was coming with that they got gave me my underwear and they both ran off with their cutlass. I got up and quickly put on my cloths as I saw a man and two children coming I guess that day a father decided to take his kids for a swim and that saved me from being raped, abused and possibly killed.

This opened my eyes more to the danger I was in and I started to wonder how was I going to get out of this !, the final straw with the escort service came when one night myself ,princess and Mary decided that we would go clubbing we were staying by one of the bosses house in five rivers, so we decided why not go out have some fun and so we dressed up and left around 9pm that faithful Friday night, we when to the club and we had a blast ,we always had fun when we went out together and that night was no different! After having the night of our lives dancing out stress ,worried and pain away, we left the club around 5:30am and took a taxi home, we had to stop out by the junction and walk in as we got out the maxi we noticed police cars, lights and commotion as we got nearer to the scene we noticed the house was riddled with him bullets, my God had we been in that house that night I would not be here writing to you.

We got away from the scene as quickly as we could without raising attention and got into a maxi to San Juan where the other house was located. I was so frightened out of my mind all I could think about from that point on was how to get out!

I started to pull away in the room I didn't want to go out on any jobs, I was scared! this life was not for me this is not what I envisioned for myself. I had to do something and fast!, so one day about two weeks after the shooting up of the other house I was in town and I bounced up on an old friend from church who was also a police officer and we got to talking I confided in him all that was happening and what I was going through to survive and to keep a roof over my head ; he was heartbroken by my story and decide to help me he said that he can arrange for them to burst the location and lock up the boss but I told him no!, since that would now put me and the other girls in danger of being hurt by the other men involved!. He understood where I was coming from an agreed not to do such instead I decided that I would let him call and threaten John since John though he played rugged he was the softest one of the men by doing that it will get him afraid and he'd allow me to go freely and that plan did work instead of me going out on jobs I was told by John that I will answer phone calls and send the girls out on jobs.

That was a better option for me at least it would get me out from being directly in the part of these perverts.

I still was not happy since I really didn't want to be a part of such a business, I didn't want to be the one causing further damage to already damaged and broken girls.
I did this for about one month while I saved up along with princess and Mary and we got ourselves a little apartment in the curepe area, and we left one day and never returned.!

 That was the start of a new beginning for all three of us.

Chapter 13

A New Beginning!!!

I was finally free, my girls and I were free! We had a chance at a fresh start, we got out healthy and alive and that was all that mattered to us, now it was up to us what we were going to do with that freedom with our breakthrough. Me I did not know what princess and Mary were thinking but all I knew was I was going to find a way to make it! to have a better life, I didn't know how but I was going to find it. The following days after we left the escort house we mostly stayed indoors for fear of being seen; but we couldn't keep staying indoors we had to make up our minds and start looking for jobs and so sucked up our fear of the unknown and got to work. That day when we had all gone looking for work surprisingly two of us for lucky, myself and princess I was ecstatic! I got through with a sales clerk position at a show store in Port-Of-Spain and princess got through at a food place serving, unfortunately Mary wasn't so lucky! she didn't find anything but that was ok! I remember saying to her we are in this together what I have is also yours to share, you see we had come from a dark place and I was not about to allow her to slip back there! Even though she eventually left us and did return to that life, I guess frustration led her back after trying to get work and she wasn't finding any.

When Mary left princess and I continued working and started planning to do courses to better ourselves, life was good.

As I continued to work as a sales girl I longed for more! I wanted more out of life , more for myself! , I didn't want to settle for just being a sales girl. So while working I continued looking for something better!.

I worked as a sales clerk for about six months before I decided to try my hand at telemarketing with a company I saw advertised in one of the local newspapers they were going to train you and you could work from the office or from home the choice was mines to make, and so I called got the interview and was ready to start working as a telemarketer! This was no easy job in fact it was harder than my sales clerk job and you had to make sales to be paid. I made a couple of sales but I quickly knew that telemarketing was not the job for me, and with that conclusion in my head I started searching again in the papers for something better than the telemarketing and to my surprise after searching the employment section for weeks I saw a vacancy for a part-time legal secretary position the requirements were just what iced my cake they wanted someone with CXC English & Office Procedures with the ability to type! And oh it was up my ally I had done three subjects as a private candidate earlier that year and passed so I was eligible to apply for the position since the firm was going to further train whoever got the position, and guess who did?! Me. I was so excited and happy life was slowly turning around positively for me.

I started my on the job training and started working as a part-time legal secretary for Mr. Sam he was a very good and kind hearted man and a great lawyer at that. Working in a lawyer's office wow' it had to all sink in from where I came, where I was, the things I had done to a legal Secretary. My tunnel days were over, sixteen years old and things were now getting better my life was now starting to make some sense. My favourite part of working in a lawyer's office was the fact that I was privileged to help people, I was always a talker, I could motivate almost anyone even though sometimes I couldn't motivate myself, I was privileged to go to the Family Court to file documents in matters my boss was working on, matters that involved children. I enjoyed my journey and experiences, I learnt so much and was introduced to a few great people along the way. If you take one thing from this I want you to take this! "NO Matter How Dark life may seem, no matter the storms raging against you, remember that there is still hope!" No storms last forever. The bible and all said though weeping may endure for a night not comes in the morning, your Morning has come.

Chapter 14

Life was looking up! Brighter days!

I worked at the law firm for six good months that year was the best year of my life! I felt good, I had a great job, a roof over my head to call home, food and of course my dreams! I enrolled to do Computerized Accounting and was accepted paid my fees and continued my journey to greatness, no one and nothing could stop me from this point on, I just kept telling myself "Ackeisha you must make it one day keep pushing", and that is exactly what I did. I kept pursuing my goals little by little one by one. I eventually my boyfriend Otis I was drawn and captivated by his eyes! and smile. He was a handsome man much older than I was but his heart was good and so were his intentions, Otis and I were great friends for a few months before it for serious and we decided to take it to the next level. By seventeen I was living with my him and life continued to be good in fact life for better I did my accounting course and passed for my certification and I was happy very happy for once. After my time was up at the lawyer's office since it was part-time I was home for a good while, I told you life was good I was being taken care of and my boyfriend had already told me he didn't want me to run up and down looking for work he'd take care of me.! Life was nice and love was good too. I didn't work for two good years within that time I was saving and planning to open my own business which was always my dream and desire since I was a little girl. I grew up around and in business so I had that desire from young at age 12yrs I had already decided that I wanted to be an entrepreneur; A business woman! And by all means I was going to make that dream a reality! By this time I was nearing my nineteenth birthday and so I decided to visit Tobago the land of my birth the place I grew up and called home! , it was an enjoyable trip back I had hope after all those years things in Tobago would have changed!, and some things did change !, there were more buildings and businesses but the mentality of the people still remained the same!, the same issues I ran from the same plague I tried to elude was still very much rampant and nothing much was still not being done to bring about and impact change!.

I visited my old friends and I even met with my mother I wanted one of their business apartments to rent in the coming months to open my very own business which was named and registered as Ackeisha's One Stop Business Centre which is now a beauty business known as Empressdarkie Beauty Empire.

I am a mother to a beautiful 6-year-old little girl and because of her I will fight to ensure that child abuse Stops and changes are made! She is my light and continued source of inspiration and hope!.

Never give up never give it that the day you give up might be the very day the good Lord had ordained for you to win! So don't let the trails define you, use the trails to build you and you define yourself!

Though my journey was bitter, dark, painful and sometimes lonely I am here! And Today I Stand! I stand to be your Voice! I Stand to be your Hope! and I Stand to say to you, that you are more than your abuse! break out and be free!.
Speak out and release the pain from deep within your soul and learn to live again!

Chronicles of a survivor

" When Silence is Broken the True Strength of a Survivor is Born! "

You can and will Survive it too!
 Don't give up! the only time you lose is if you give in and quit!
You got God Fight In you! he will surely bring you through!
No test no testimony.

Chapter 15

Short Poem titled - Surviving the pain!

Purpose from pain!

God has a purpose for your pain, your pain wasn't in Vain!

I know you feel slain, every day is constant pain,

your tears fall like the rain, and sometimes you even feel shame

But your pains are not in vain,

You won't Die in this sick twisted game

Where the abuser cast Blame to make you feel shame,

Like you going insane!

Oh No You Won't Die in this Sick twisted game! That inflicted so much pain!
There's purpose for your pain and soon you will reign.!!!

Written by: Ackeisha Kent
#I Stand #I Survived #Chroniclesofasurvivor

"When Silence is Broken the True Strength of a Woman is Born
"

We all suffered that pain, in different ways,

We had been denied the right to be a child, to take our times to grow, we lived the night's and day's in fear; but against all odds we Survived!
We are more than victims we are Survivors!

"When Silence is Broken the True Strength of a Survivor is Born "!

We must stand now!

I believe if we must fight against this dreaded issue plaguing our children we must first understand what we are fighting against, so many of us does not know exactly what is child abuse, there are so many misconceptions about this topic/issue that one cannot begin to create or foster change if one is not educated on the issue so as to understand what it is, and the damages that it causes to its victims. Let's look at what is child abuse below.

What is child abuse?

Child Abuse is signs of trauma which can include but are not limited to physical, sexual or emotional maltreatment of a child under the age of eighteen.
This can result in harm, or potentially cause harm to the child.

threats to harm the child weather acted upon or not is also child abuse.

Child abuse can take place in a child's home schools or communities of which the child lives.
Child Abuse is more often times committed by individuals close to the child or the child's family. Beware! !!

Types of abuse:

Sexual Abuse
Sexual molestation

Physical Abuse

Emotional or Psychological Abuse

Neglect

"When Silence is Broken the true Strength of a Survivor is Born

"

Chronicles of A Survivor

When Silence is Broken the true Strength of a Survivor is Born!

" - A. Kent

STOP CHILD ABUSE NOW!

A Few Abuse Facts!!

- 90% of the time the victim knows his/her abuser
- A child or victim of abuse may only reach out once for help and if ignored or denied may never speak out

about the abuse again! This is very bad for the victim! Try to be a good listener!

- Victims may not speak out because of Fear!
- Children who are left unsupervised in public places or at home are at risk of being abused in one form or another, please be aware of who you leave children with and teach your children what is good and bad touch so they can identify it when someone tries it.

Chronicles of A Survivor – Ackeisha Kimberly Kent

When silence is broken the true strength of a Survivor is Born!

30509817R00031

Printed in Great Britain
by Amazon